CW00968533

TAE KWON-DO

Green Belt to Red Belt

The Official Tae Kwon-do Association
of Great Britain Training Manual

Produced by the Senior Instructors
of the TAGB

A & C Black · London

First published 1997 by
A & C Black (Publishers) Ltd
35 Bedford Row, London WC1R 4JH

Copyright © 1997 by Tae Kwon-do International Ltd

ISBN 0 7136 4611 X

A CIP catalogue record for this book
is available from the British Library.

Distributed in the USA by
The Talman Company
131 Spring Street
New York, NY 10012

Designed and typeset by
Alan Hamp @ Design for Books.

Printed and bound in Great Britain by
Hillman Printers (Frome) Ltd, Frome, Somerset

Acknowledgements

All photographs by
Martin Sellars.

Thanks to Dave Oliver,
Ron Sergiew, Kenny Walton,
Mike Dew, Paul Donnelly and
Gianni Peros for taking part
in the demonstrations.

Thanks to David Mitchell for
helping with the text.

Contents

Introduction

The Tae Kwon-do Association of Great Britain (TAGB) was founded in 1983 and it is now the largest single tae kwon-do body in Britain. It is a member of the British Tae Kwon-do Council (BTC), tae kwon-do's umbrella organisation approved by the Sports Council. Not only does the TAGB enjoy formidable representation on the BTC, but its members are widely regarded as amongst the most successful competitors in just about any martial arena, whether under points, semi-contact or full contact rules.

The TAGB is a founder member of Tae Kwon-do International, the world governing body for all forms of tae kwon-do practice.

The TAGB practises tae kwon-do deriving from the *Chang Hun* style, originated and developed by that most influential of early international tae kwon-do pioneers, General Choi Hong Hi.

The first volume in this series – *White Belt to Yellow Belt* – contains many of the techniques to which this second volume refers. It is therefore essential that you familiarise yourself with what has gone before.

In this second volume we will be tracing the grading requirements for Green Belt, Blue Belt and Red Belt (6th kup to 1st kup).

Also available in the series is *The Black Belt Syllabus*, covering first and second Dans.

All queries regarding the practice of tae kwon-do should be sent to the TAGB, Redfield Leisure Centre, 163A Church Road, Redfield, Bristol BS5 9LA (tel: 0117 955 1046).

The six belt colours of tae kwon-do

Tae kwon-do is a structured martial art, based on a syllabus designed to introduce students gradually to the skills of tae kwon-do; the stage that a student has reached at any time is reflected in the colour of the belt worn. The following belt colours are used within the TAGB.

White signifies a stage of innocence such as that of the novice student with no previous knowledge of tae kwon-do.

Yellow signifies the earth from which the plant sprouts and takes root, as the foundations of tae kwon-do are laid.

Green symbolises the growth of the plant as tae kwon-do skills begin to develop.

Blue symbolises heaven, towards which the plant is growing as it matures, reflecting the progression of tae kwon-do training.

Red represents potential danger, cautioning the student to exercise control and warning the opponent to beware!

Black is the opposite of white, signifying both maturity and proficiency. It also symbolises the wearer's imperviousness to darkness and fear.

Green Belt (6th kup)

6th kup introduces three new stances, three new strikes, a new punch and four new blocks.

Closed ready stance 'A'
(moa junbi sogi 'A')

The first stance we encounter in this grade is a new ready stance (see **fig. 7** on page 14). Known as closed ready stance 'A', the feet are together and both hands are brought to the chest. The right hand clenches into a fist while the left hand envelops it in a symbolic representation of the juxtaposition of hard and soft/internal and external energy.

Inward knife hand strike/ middle side punch from fixed stance
(anuro sonkal taerigi/yop jirugi from gojung sogi)

Fig. 1 Inward knife hand strike uses the little finger edge of the hand in a chopping action on a target such as the side of the opponent's neck. Use twin forearm block against the opponent's obverse punch. Then bring your left fist against the right shoulder to help power knife hand to the side of the opponent's neck.

Fig. 2 Twist your hips in a clockwise direction as your left foot slides forward into a fixed stance. Fixed stance is rather like a longer L-stance, where bodyweight shifts forward until it is carried 50/50 on both feet. Use hip twist and bodyweight shift, coupled with the long pull back and spasm-closing of the right hand, to inject power into a middle side punch.

Bending ready stance
(guburyo junbi sogi)

Fig. 3 Bending ready
stance is a transient
position – held for the
shortest instant – during
which one foot is lifted
high and the knee cocked
ready to deliver a kick.

Fig. 4 The heel and edge
of the right foot is then
thrust powerfully into the
opponent's mid-
section in a side kick
(yop chagi).

Middle side elbow strike
(yop palkup)
This is a short range strike using the point of your elbow against a person standing
behind you. Transfer your bodyweight over your right foot and take up right
L-stance. Look over your right shoulder and drive the elbow back into the opponent's solar plexus. Reinforce the strike by pushing your right fist back with your
left palm (see **fig. 45** on page 29).

Knee strike
(moorup)
Knee strike is a devastating short range strike to the opponent's front of thigh, groin,
solar plexus or head/face. Grab the opponent by his shoulders and jerk his upper
body forward and down. Hold him firmly as you drive the knee into his solar plexus
(see **fig. 48** on page 31).

Circular block
(dollimyo makgi)

Circular block is an inner forearm technique that takes the inside of the forearm down and up, across the body, scooping and lifting the opponent's attacking technique.

Fig. 5 The opponent attempts front kick. Guard your face with your left fist and bring the right fist down and across your body, thumb-side toward the opponent's leg. Draw back your left fist and strongly rotate your hips behind the block, catching the opponent's Achilles tendon and lifting and deflecting his kick.

Fig. 6 Because of its wide circling path, circular block is quite capable of knocking the opponent's kick to one side and then carrying on up to intercept his following punch.

Upward palm block
(sonbadak ollyo makgi)

Upward palm block deflects the incoming technique such that an attacking punch is lifted and the ribs are exposed to a follow-up (see **fig. 43** on page 28). A kick can also be lifted by upward palm block and the attacker unbalanced.

Waist block
(hori makgi)

Waist block uses a circling action of the arm to bat an incoming technique to the side. Take up left L-stance and middle forearm guarding block. The opponent performs a left middle turning kick and you respond by drawing back your left fist and using that action to help power an outward/downward travelling forearm block that strikes the opponent's shin with the little finger edge of your forearm (see **fig. 44** on page 29).

X-fist pressing block
(kyocha noollo makgi)

X-fist is formed when both fists are thrust out with the thumbs facing upward such that the forearms cross each other. The 'v' between the two fists is capable of trapping an incoming technique and bringing it to a stop. Thus, the opponent performs a right front kick and you slide your left foot forward into walking stance (it is important that you close the distance). Draw both your fists back, palm upward facing to your hip, and thrust them out and down, taking the opponent's rising shin between them. Block well out from your body (see **fig. 46** on page 30).

Won Hyo

The pattern required for 6th kup is Won Hyo, though you must also be prepared to perform any or all of the earlier patterns.

Won Hyo is the name of the Silla Dynasty monk who reputedly introduced Zen Buddhism to Korea in AD 686. This form contains 28 movements arranged in the following pattern:

Fig. 7 Begin from closed ready stance 'A', with your feet pressed firmly together.

❶ **Fig. 8** Move your left foot 90° to the left, stepping smoothly into a right L-stance and performing a twin forearm block.

❷ **Fig. 9** Without changing your stance, perform a high inward right knife hand strike, at the same time drawing back your left fist to your right shoulder.

❸ **Fig. 10** *Above, right.* Lengthen your stance by sliding your left foot forward into fixed stance. Draw back your right hand, using this action to help power a left middle side punch.

❹ **Fig. 11** Draw your left foot to the right, cross your forearms in front of your chest and then step 180° with the right foot into left L-stance as you perform a twin forearm block.

❺ **Fig. 12** Perform high inward-travelling left knife hand as you bring your right fist against your left shoulder.

❻ **Fig. 13** *Below, left.* Change to fixed stance by sliding your right foot forward and perform right middle side punch.

❼ **Fig. 14** *Below, right.* Bring the right foot to the left and take both your arms back.

❼ *cont.* **Fig. 15** Lift your left foot into a right bending ready stance 'A' and make a forearm guarding block.

❽ **Fig. 16** Thrust out your left foot in a middle side piercing kick.

❾ **Fig. 17** Drop the spent foot forward into a right L-stance and, as you do, perform middle knife hand guarding block.

⓾ Fig. 18 Step forward with your right foot into left L-stance as you perform a second middle knife hand guarding block.

⓫ Fig. 19 Now step forward with your left foot into a right L-stance and perform a third middle knife hand guarding block.

⓬ Fig. 20 Step forward with your right foot, this time taking up right walking stance. As you do, perform a right middle thrust with extended fingers and bring your left hand under your right elbow.

13 **Fig. 21** Step around 90° anti-clock-wise with your left foot and cross your forearms in front of your chest.

13 *cont.* **Fig. 22** *Above, right.* Slide your left foot forward into a right L-stance and perform a twin forearm block.

14 **Fig. 23** Perform a high inward knife hand strike with your right hand even as you draw back the left fist to the front of your left shoulder.

⓯ Fig. 24 Slide your left foot forward into fixed stance and thrust out a left middle side punch.

⓰ Fig. 25 *Below, left.* Draw your left foot to the right and cross your forearms in front of your chest. Slide your right foot out by 180° into left L-stance and perform a twin forearm block.

⓱ Fig. 26 *Below.* Perform another inward-travelling knife hand strike, this time with the left as the right fist is pulled back to the left shoulder.

🔞 **Fig. 27** Slide your right foot forward into fixed stance and thrust out a right middle side punch.

🔞 **Fig. 28** *Above, right.* Bring your right foot to the left and extend your left palm down in front of you.

🔞 *cont.* **Fig. 29** Step forward with the left foot into walking stance and turn your upper body 90° to the right. Bring your right forearm forward and perform a circular block. Power for this block is generated by the fast-withdrawing left hand which spasms into a fist as the block is focused.

20 **Fig. 30** Maintain your guard and relax your shoulders as you perform a right low front snap kick.

21 **Fig. 31** *Below, left.* Lower the spent foot carefully into a walking stance – don't flop down with it! Perform left middle reverse punch.

22 **Fig. 32** *Below.* Bring your left hand back as you guard with the right and perform left inner forearm circular block without moving forward.

㉓ **Fig. 33** Hold your guard steady as you perform low front snap kick with your left foot.

㉔ **Fig. 34** *Above, right.* Drop the spent foot carefully into left walking stance and perform right middle reverse punch.

㉕ **Fig. 35** Bring your right foot forward and up into a left bending ready stance 'A', while taking up a forearm guarding block.

㉖ Fig. 36 Thrust out your right foot in a middle side piercing kick.

㉗ Fig. 37 Lower the right foot and turn 90° anti-clockwise, allowing both arms to lag behind.

27 *cont.* **Fig. 38** Step out with the left foot into right L-stance and perform a middle guarding block with the left forearm.

28 **Fig. 39** Bring your left foot to the right and allow your arms to lag behind. Then slide your right foot 180° to the right and into left L-stance. Accompany this movement with a middle forearm guarding block and *kihap*.

Conclude Won Hyo by drawing the right foot back into closed ready stance 'A'.

Three-step semi-free sparring (intermediate)

We performed elementary three-step semi-free sparring for 7th kup and it is continued into this grade, although no fixed routines are taught. The opponent selects three attacks – punches and/or kicks – while you block each in turn and decisively counter attack with *kihap* on the last. These sequences must be demonstrated on both left and right sides and, though choice of techniques is left to the candidates, you should be aware that you are now expected to demonstrate a level of skill commensurate with your grade. Be prepared to demonstrate three-step semi-free sparring sequences.

Two-step sparring
(ibo matsoki)

Two-step sparring is similar to the three-step variety we encountered in the lower kup grades. However, in this version, more advanced techniques are used and the attacker performs just two prearranged techniques. The attacker always begins from right L-stance and forearm guarding block, and the defender from parallel ready stance. The defender blocks the first attack and counters the second with *kihap* to complete the sequence.

Two-step sparring (1)

Fig. 40 In the first of the four two-step sparring sequences required for 6th kup, both attacker and defender take up parallel ready stances. Then the attacker makes *kihap* and takes up right L-stance while the defender stands waiting. The defender makes *kihap* as a ready signal and the attacker steps forward into right walking stance and thrusts out a right high obverse punch. Step back into right walking stance and take the punch on your left forearm in a rising block.

26

Fig. 41 The attacker draws back his right fist and brings his left knee up and forward in a front kick. Respond by drawing back both your elbows and thrusting them out in X-fist pressing block to the attacker's shin.

Fig. 42 The attacker drops forward onto his left foot. You pull back both your fists and then thrust them out once more in a high twin punch to his cheekbones. *Kihap* at this point. The impact of your fists is made stronger by the attacker's own forward movement.

Two-step sparring (2)

Begin as for sequence (1) above.

Fig. 43 The attacker takes a short step forward into left fixed stance and performs a middle side punch. Respond by stepping back from ready stance into right L-stance and deflect his punch with upward palm block.

Fig. 44 The attacker pulls his right fist back, turning clockwise on his right foot, and performs left turning kick to mid-section. Respond by stepping back into left L-stance and blocking down with a right waist block.

Fig. 45 The attacker's spent foot drops forward, bringing him into range of your side elbow middle strike. *Kihap* at this point.

Two-step sparring (3)

Fig. 46 Begin as usual. This time the attacker launches a right middle front kick. Step back into left walking stance and perform an X-fist pressing block against the fast rising shin. Don't forget to block well out from your body.

30

Fig. 47 The attacker drops forward into left walking stance, thrusting out both his fists in a twin high punch. Respond by stepping back into right walking stance, withdrawing your fists to your hips and thrusting out/rotating them into wedging block.

Fig. 48 Having deflected the attacker's twin punch, reach forward and take hold of his shoulders, pull his upper body down and perform a left knee strike into his solar plexus. *Kihap* and drop your left leg back into stance once more.

Two-step sparring (4)

Fig. 49 Begin as usual. The attacker steps forward into right walking stance and thrusts out his right fingertips in a high section flat thrust. Respond by stepping back with your right foot and performing a rising block with knife hand.

Fig. 50 The attacker puts weight over his right foot, drawing the left knee up and into a middle side piercing kick. Respond by stepping back into left L-stance and parrying the kick with an inward palm block. The amount of leverage you apply to the end of the attacker's kicking leg is sufficient to spin him away from you.

Fig. 51 Counter attack with a front kick to the attacker's coccyx.

Fig. 52 Land forward and perform twin punch to the opponent's kidneys. *Kihap* at this point.

Free sparring
(jayoo matsoki)

Fig. 53 Free sparring begins at this grade and continues through the TAGB syllabus. Free sparring involves the unprogrammed exchange of techniques between two partners. As a concession to safety, sparring partners must wear approved protective equipment in the form of boots, mitts and head guards. However, the wearing of such equipment does not mean you can use full-power techniques! You are expected to control the impact of your techniques at all times and the protection is only there in case of an accident.

You must:
- wear only approved protective equipment
- spar only under the direction of a properly qualified person
- obey that person's directions
- take proper care for your own safety
- use only techniques at which you are competent.

You must not:
- wear spectacles, jewellery or unauthorised protective equipment
- attack the groin or the throat
- attack the face with open hand techniques
- use excessive force in technique application
- attack the opponent's joints
- sweep the opponent's feet away
- grapple with the opponent.

Fig. 54 Encourage each other by providing openings and acknowledging an effective technique with a friendly nod. That way, your free sparring will be an enjoyable experience and it will not deteriorate into meaningless brawling.

If you begin to feel intimidated, withdraw and wait for the instructor to notice – but do not leave the sparring area without permission.

Green Belt (5th kup)

5th kup introduces a new stance, a new strike, a new kick and four new blocks.

X-stance
(kyocha sogi)

X-stance is an upright posture used as you close with the opponent. Jump forward and land with your right foot tucked behind the left. Your right shin presses against your left calf and your right heel is lifted (see **fig. 116** on page 59). Use the energy of the jump to add power to a high side strike with your left back fist to the opponent's temple.

Front elbow strike
(palkup)

Fig. 55 Front elbow is a powerful close-range strike, using hip action to drive the point of your elbow into the opponent's sternum (breast bone). It is important to concentrate impact over the point of the elbow and not along the length of the forearm. Slide forward with your left foot and take up walking stance, using this movement to help power the strike.

Reverse turning kick
(bandae dollyo chagi)

Reverse turning kick uses a circular action that brings the heel into contact with the target anywhere from the groin upward. Begin from right L-stance by twisting your head clockwise to look over your right shoulder. Allow your left heel to rise as both feet swivel (see **fig. 111** on page 57).

Bring your right foot up and back, lifting the heel into the side of the opponent's head in a high reverse circling action (see **fig. 112** on page 57).

Twin knife hand block
(sang sonkal makgi)

Fig. 56 Twin knife hand block is used against simultaneous attacks. It is performed in exactly the same way as twin outer forearm block on pages 92–3 of *White Belt to Yellow Belt* (volume one of the series). Begin from right L-stance by drawing your left arm across your chest so the right arm overlies the left. The left arm moves across the front and rotates palm-down to block a right punch while the right lifts and rotates little finger-uppermost to deflect a downward-travelling side fist strike.

Palm heel hooking block
(golcho makgi)

Fig. 57 Palm heel hooking block uses the palm to deflect the opponent's technique. If required, the fingers can curl around and grab the opponent's wrist and the technique then turns into a grasping block (*butjaba makgi*). By this means, the opponent can be pulled forward off balance.

Double forearm block
(doo palmok makgi)

Fig. 58 This is a very powerful forearm block in which both arms are swung up together, generating a great deal of force. Slide your left foot forward into walking stance, turn your hips strongly into the technique and block with the thumb-side of your left forearm. Your right fist is brought close to the left elbow.

Twin straight forearm block
(sang sun palmok)

This is a very powerful block using the little finger-side of both forearms to stop the opponent's turning or reverse turning kick to mid- or high section. The opponent attempts a high right turning kick and you move into and onto the technique from sitting stance. Note the correct angle of stance, allowing your right forearm to check the attacker's knee, and the left his instep/ankle (see **fig. 105** on page 54).

37

Yul Gok

Yul Gok is the pseudonym of the great sixteenth century philosopher and scholar Yi I (AD1536–1584), nicknamed 'The Confucius Of Korea'. The pattern's 38 moves refer to his birthplace on latitude 38° and the diagram represents the scholar.

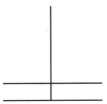

Begin from parallel ready stance.

❶ Fig. 59 *Above.* Move your left foot to the left and let your right fist move away from your side. Drop into sitting stance and pull your right fist back to your hip. Even as you are pulling back your right fist, extend the left slowly at chest height and bring it into your own mid-line. (This is the measuring fist which we first came across in the three-step sparring sequence (4), on page 102 of volume one). **❷** Then punch quickly to the mid-section with your right fist.

❸ Fig. 60 *Left.* Quickly pull back your right fist, using this energy to help thrust out a left middle punch. The right and left punches must follow each other quickly.
❹ Bring the left foot to the right then step out to the right with your right foot, settling into a second sitting stance. Extend your right fist slowly into the mid-line.
❺ Pull your right fist back strongly and thrust out the left into a mid-section punch.
❻ Pull back the left fist and punch with the right. These two punches follow each other very quickly.

❼ **Fig. 61** Bring your left foot to the right and bring your right arm back across your chest so your left fist overlies your right forearm.

❼ *cont.* **Fig. 62** *Above, right.* Step forward 45° with your right foot into right walking stance, at the same time performing a high right inner forearm block.

❽ **Fig. 63** Keep your hands in the same position and perform a low left snap kick.

❾ Fig. 64 Drop the spent left foot forward into a second walking stance and use the energy of your body movement during landing to help power a left middle obverse punch.

❿ Fig. 65 *Above, right.* Pull back your left fist, using the energy of this movement to help power a right middle reverse punch.

⓫ Fig. 66 Draw your left foot back and take your left arm across your chest so your right fist overlies the left forearm.

⓫ *cont.* **Fig. 67** Slide the left foot diagonally out to the left at a 90° angle while performing a high inner forearm block with the left arm.

⓬ **Fig. 68** *Above, right.* Keep your arms still as you snap kick to the opponent's knee or groin with your right foot.

⓭ **Fig. 69** Carefully drop the spent right foot into walking stance and use the energy of landing to help power a right middle obverse punch.

⑭ Fig. 70 Pull your right fist back strongly, using this action to help power a left middle reverse punch.

⑮ Fig. 71 *Below, left.* Draw your right foot back and move your open right hand, palm inward, near to your left ear. Your left fist is to the outside of the right forearm and the palm is rotated away from your face.

⑮ *cont.* **Fig. 72** *Below.* Twist your hips clockwise and slide the leading right foot 45° to the right so you take up a new right walking stance. Pull back your left fist to your side, using this action to help power a high hooking block with your right palm.

16 **Fig. 73** Remain in the same stance as you bring your left hip forward. At the same time, draw back your right hand and close it into a fist. Use this action to help power a second high hooking block with the left palm.

17 **Fig. 74** *Above, right.* Pull back your left hand and perform a powerful right middle obverse punch.

18 **Fig. 75** Now step forward with your left foot into left walking stance and draw back your right fist. At the same time, perform a high hooking block with your left palm.

⑲ Fig. 76 Bring your right hip forward, withdraw your left hand and perform a fourth high hooking block, this time using the right palm.

⑳ Fig. 77 Quickly pull your right hand back to your side and close it into a fist. Use this action to help power a left middle obverse punch.

㉑ Fig. 78 Step forward into a right walking stance while pulling your left fist back and performing a right middle obverse punch.

❷❷ Fig. 79 Pull your right fist back and extend your left elbow to take up a guard as you simultaneously bring your left foot up and forward into right bending ready stance 'A'.

❷❸ Fig. 80 *Above, right.* Thrust your left foot out in a side piercing kick to mid-section.

❷❹ Fig. 81 Drop the spent left foot in a forward position and begin turning your right hip toward the front. Open your left hand so the thumb is uppermost and make ready a right elbow strike. Then twist your right hip fully forward, so you are in left walking stance. Use this hip twisting action to help drive the point of your right elbow into the palm of your left hand.

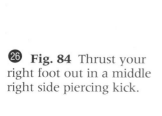 **Fig. 82** Step across to the right with your left leg and twist your body 180° clockwise. Take both arms out behind you in preparation for taking up a guard.

25 *cont.* **Fig. 83** *Above, right.* Bring your arms into guarding position and lift your right foot as you take up left side bending ready stance 'A'.

26 **Fig. 84** Thrust your right foot out in a middle right side piercing kick.

27 **Fig. 85** Drop your right foot into right walking stance. Smack the point of your left elbow into the palm of your right hand.

28 **Fig. 86** *Above, right.* Bring your left foot forward and begin sliding it 90° to the left. Fold your left arm across your chest so the palm of your open left hand comes to lie in front of your right cheek. Your right arm folds around the outside of the left, with the fingers pointing in the direction of your slide.

28 *cont.* **Fig. 87** Complete the slide into right L-stance and perform a twin knife hand block.

㉙ **Fig. 88** Step through with the right foot into right walking stance and perform a right middle spear finger thrust. The left back hand is brought underneath your right elbow.

㉚ **Fig. 89** *Above, right.* Step right back with your right foot and turn 180° clockwise. Fold both arms across your chest.

㉚ *cont.* **Fig. 90** Slide your right foot forward and take up a left L-stance. At the same time, perform a twin knife hand block.

31 **Fig. 91** Step through with the left foot into left walking stance and perform a left middle straight spear finger thrust. The back of your right hand is below your left elbow.

32 **Fig. 92** *Below, left.* Slide your left foot back and to your left and fold your arms across your upper body, left inside right.

32 *cont.* **Fig. 93** *Below.* Slide your left foot forward at 90° and drop into left walking stance. At the same time, perform a high left outer block.

㉝ Fig. 94 *Far left.* Pull back your blocking arm and thrust out a right middle reverse punch.

㉞ Fig. 95 *Left.* Step forward with your right foot into walking stance. At the same time, perform a high right outer block.

㉟ Fig. 96 *Right.* Pull back your blocking arm and thrust out a left middle reverse punch.

㊱ Fig. 97 *Far right.* Jump forward, coming to a stop in left X-stance. Use the energy of motion and the pulling back of your right arm to help power a high side strike with the back of your left fist.

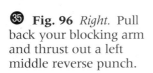

37 **Fig. 98** Turn 90° clockwise and take both arms to your left.

37 *cont.* **Fig. 99** *Below, left.* Slide your right foot forward into walking stance. Swing both arms up in a right high double forearm block.

38 **Fig. 100** *Below.* Bring your right foot to the left, trail both arms to your right and look to your left. Then slide your left foot out into left walking stance and perform a second high double forearm block. *Kihap* at this point.

Draw back your left foot and resume ready stance once more.

Semi-free sparring (advanced)

The semi-free sparring requirement for 5th kup is three advanced sequences using difficult techniques to show your current level of ability. Remember that you must perform these techniques on both sides.

Two-step sparring

A further four two-step sparring sequences are required for this grade.

Two-step sparring (5)

Begin from parallel ready stance.

Fig. 101 The attacker steps back into right L-stance and makes *kihap* while you answer with *kihap* to signify that you are ready. Then the attacker spins clockwise and you draw your right foot back into right L-stance. Extend your left hand ready to block.

Fig. 102 Bring your left palm down in a waist block, adopting a circular action to deflect the attacker's foot to his right.

Fig. 103 The attacker lands, then steps forward into left walking stance and attempts a high section palm strike to your face. Step back into left L-stance and deflect the thrust with inward moving forearm block.

Fig. 104 Slide your right foot to the outside of the attacker's left and take up walking stance. Bring your left hip forward and strike under the attacker's left arm, applying a reverse knife hand to his solar plexus. *Kihap* at this point.

Two-step sparring (6)

Fig. 105 The opponent attempts a high right turning kick and you respond by taking your left leg back into sitting stance, checking the kick with twin straight forearm block.

54

Fig. 106 The attacker lands and then steps forward into left walking stance, thrusting out a high left arc hand (*bandal son*). The object in such a strike might be to grasp your windpipe, so step back quickly into right L-stance and deflect the arc hand with a left palm heel hooking block.

Fig. 107 Curl your fingers and thumb around his forearm and pull his left hand toward you. Pick up your left foot and thrust it out in a middle side kick. *Kihap* at this point.

Two-step sparring (7)

Fig. 108 The attacker steps forward into right fixed stance and attempts a high right side fist. Pull back your left foot into L-stance and block the attack with twin outer forearm block.

Fig. 109 *Above, right.* The attacker then slides his right foot to the left and begins to twist his hips anti-clockwise, lifting the left foot. He looks over his left shoulder and sees you step toward him.

Fig. 110 The attacker continues turning, straightening his left knee and swinging it back at middle height in a reverse turning kick. Evade the incoming heel by sliding back and guarding with knife hand.

Fig. 111 Twist clockwise on your left foot and look over your right shoulder.

Fig. 112 Bring your right foot up and back, reverse circling the heel into the side of the opponent's head in a high reverse turning kick. *Kihap* at this point and retrieve the kick.

Two-step sparring (8)

Fig. 113 The attacker thrusts out right middle side piercing kick and you respond by stepping back with your right foot and deflecting the kick with the thumb-side of your forearm in a waist block.

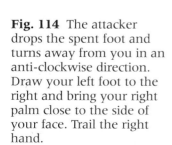

Fig. 114 The attacker drops the spent foot and turns away from you in an anti-clockwise direction. Draw your left foot to the right and bring your right palm close to the side of your face. Trail the right hand.

Fig. 115 The attacker slides his left foot back and attempts a high left knife hand strike which you stop with knife hand guarding block.

Fig. 116 *Below.* Jump forward into X-stance, crossing your right foot behind the left and flexing your knees. As you land, deliver a high back fist strike against the attacker's temple. *Kihap* at this point and then withdraw.

Free sparring

Free sparring is a requirement for this grade and you are expected to have shown an improvement in selection and usage of technique.

Blue Belt (4th kup)

4th kup introduces three new stances, one new strike, three punches and four blocks. There is also a release from wrist grab which is taken from the pattern Joon Gun.

Closed ready stance 'B'
(moa junbi sogi 'B')

Fig. 117 In this upright stance the feet are pressed firmly together and both hands are in front of the solar plexus. The open left hand envelops the right fist.

Rear foot stance
(dwit bal sogi)
This is a short stance in which the front foot is no more than a shoulder-width ahead of the trailing foot. The lead foot points slightly inward while the trailing foot is turned out almost at a right angle. Bend your rear knee until it overlies the toes and bend the front knee, raising the heel from the floor. Most of your bodyweight is carried over the rear foot (see **fig. 131** on page 67).

Low stance
(nachuo sogi)
Think of low stance as a walking stance extended by six inches or so. The hips are forward-facing. Low stance is useful for injecting bodyweight into a forward movement.

Rising elbow strike
(wi palkup taerigi)

Fig. 118 Rising elbow strike is a devastating short range weapon used to attack the opponent's chin. Step forward into left walking stance and swing the point of your right elbow upward, driving the opponent's head back.

Twin vertical punch
(sang sewo jirugi)

Fig. 119 We encountered this technique briefly in the previous grade. As its name implies, twin vertical punch delivers two blows simultaneously, in this case to the opponent's cheekbones. Draw both elbows back as you slide into right walking stance. Then twist your hips to the front and thrust both fists out. Notice how the fists do not corkscrew fully into the customary knuckles-upward position.

Upset punch
(dwijibo jirugi)

Upset punch is a short range technique which impacts while the elbow is still close to your own body. Step inside the opponent's right middle punch, lean to the right and take up vertical stance. Pull your left arm into a guarding position across your chest and deliver a short, jolting upset punch into the opponent's solar plexus (see **fig. 177** on page 85).

Twin upset punch
(sang dwijibo jirugi)

Fig. 120 Twin upset punch is simply two upset punches delivered simultaneously. Slide forward into left walking stance, drawing back both elbows. Then turn your hips forward and thrust your fists into the opponent's solar plexus, using the forward slide and hip twist to add energy to the impact.

Reverse knife hand block
(sonkal dung makgi)

Fig. 121 Reverse knife hand block uses the thumb-side or 'ridge' of the hand edge to deflect the opponent's technique. Begin by sliding back into right L-stance. The right hand pulls back and clenches tightly into a fist as the left moves the opposite way in a windscreen wiper-like action, rotating palm upward as contact is made with the opponent's technique.

Rising X-block
(kyocha joomuk chookyo makgi)

Fig. 122 Rising X-block uses both forearms to fend off descending attacks. Slide back with your right foot into walking stance and draw both elbows back to your hips. Use the energy of your moving body and hip twist to thrust both fists up the front of your body, rotating them so the palms are turned down. The opponent's descending knife hand strike is caught in the 'v' formed by the twin forearms.

Palm pressing block
(sonbadak noollo makgi)

Fig. 123 Palm pressing block thrusts downward to interrupt the opponent's technique at an early stage, preventing it from developing fully. The opponent punches and kicks simultaneously. Slide forward with your left foot into walking stance, your right palm thrusting down and pressing on the opponent's fast rising shin. Your left hand simultaneously rises in an upward palm block.

U-shaped block
(mongdungi makgi)

Fig. 124 U-shaped block is designed to work against an opponent armed with a pole. Slide forward with your left leg into fixed stance, blocking the pole with the reverse knife hand. The pole is then jammed against the opponent's body.

64

Release from grab

Fig. 125 The pattern Joon Gun features an effective and simple release from a wrist grab.

Fig. 126 Simply twist your hips strongly in a clockwise direction, drawing your elbow down and across your body. At the same time, rotate your left forearm so your palm is facing upward. This sudden and powerful action levers against the opponent's thumb, causing him to release his grip.

The release may be followed by a powerful counter attack such as high reverse punch. Simply swivel your hips back toward the opponent and pull the freed hand back to your hip. Use this action to help power the punch.

Joon Gun

The pattern Joon Gun is named after the Korean patriot An-Joong-gun who assassinated the first Japanese governor of Korea, Hiro Bumi Ito. The pattern consists of 32 movements, corresponding to An's age when he was executed in the Lui-Shung prison during 1910. The pattern has the following form:

Begin from closed ready stance 'B'.

❶ **Fig. 127** Slide the left foot to the left and take up right L-stance. At the same time, perform a middle side block with left reverse knife hand.

❷ **Fig. 128** Maintain the position of your hands as you draw your weight back over your right foot and lift your left knee.

❷ *cont.* **Fig. 129** Perform a left low front snap kick.

❸ **Fig. 130** *Below, left.* Drop the left foot and step forward with the right into a left rear foot stance. Turn your left hand palm downward and trail the right.

❸ *cont.* **Fig. 131** *Below.* Strongly pull back your left hand, closing it into a fist at your hip. Use this action to help power an upward block with your right palm.

❹ **Fig. 132** Bring your right foot around clockwise and fold your right hand arm across your chest with the palm downward. Extend your left fist over the top of the right upper arm.

❹ *cont.* **Fig. 133** Slide out your right foot and take up a left L-stance. Powerfully draw back your left fist and perform middle side block with right reverse knife hand.

5 **Fig. 134** Pull your bodyweight back over your left foot and perform a low right snap kick, keeping your arms exactly as they are.

6 **Fig. 135** *Below, left.* Drop the right foot and step forward with the left into a right rear foot stance. Perform a second upward palm block, this time with the left hand.

7 **Fig. 136** *Below.* Slide the left foot across and turn anti-clockwise. Bring your left palm to your right cheek and trail the right high behind you.

❼ *cont.* **Fig. 137** Slide your left foot forward into right L-stance while performing a middle guarding block with knife hand.

❽ **Fig. 138** Take up walking stance by sliding the left foot out. Extend your left elbow, close the right hand into a fist and draw it back. Then pull your left hand back and close it into a fist. Twist your hips anti-clockwise and swing your right elbow up in a high rising strike.

❾ **Fig. 139** Step forward with your right foot into left L-stance while performing a middle guarding block with knife hand.

10 **Fig. 140** *Above, left.* Slide the right foot diagonally forward into walking stance and swing your left elbow up in a high rising strike.

11 **Fig. 141** *Above.* Step forward with your left foot and turn your hips clockwise. Bring both fists to your sides, turning them palm upward.

11 *cont* **Fig. 142** Twist your hips forward, using this energy to thrust out high twin vertical punch.

12 **Fig. 143** Step forward into right walking stance and turn your hips anti-clockwise. Draw both fists to your sides, turning them palm downward.

12 *cont.* **Fig. 144** Twist your hips clockwise, using this action to help power twin upset punch.

13 **Fig. 145** Slide your right foot across and turn anti-clockwise.

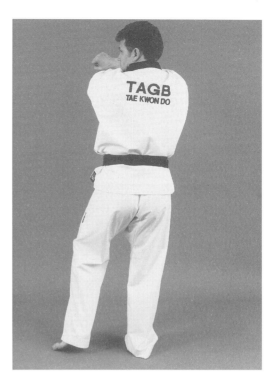

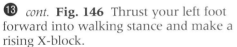 **13** *cont.* **Fig. 146** Thrust your left foot forward into walking stance and make a rising X-block.

14 **Fig. 147** *Above, right.* Draw your left foot back and cross your arms in front of your chin.

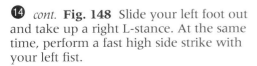 **14** *cont.* **Fig. 148** Slide your left foot out and take up a right L-stance. At the same time, perform a fast high side strike with your left fist.

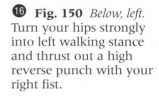 **Fig. 149** Move your left foot diagonally outward and twist your left fist anti-clockwise in a releasing move, until the knuckles face toward the floor.

16 **Fig. 150** *Below, left.* Turn your hips strongly into left walking stance and thrust out a high reverse punch with your right fist.

17 **Fig. 151** *Below.* Turn clockwise and bring your left foot to the right, crossing your forearms in front of your chin.

17 *cont.* **Fig. 152** Step out with the right foot and take up left L-stance. At the same time, perform a fast high side strike with your right fist.

18 **Fig. 153** *Above, right.* Slide your right foot diagonally outward and twist your body anti-clockwise in a releasing move, turning your right fist clockwise until the knuckles face the floor.

19 **Fig. 154** Twist your hips strongly in a clockwise direction and thrust out a high reverse punch with your left fist.

20 **Fig. 155** Bring your right foot to the left, then turn 90° anti-clockwise. Trail both arms behind you with the knuckles turned upward.

20 *cont.* **Fig. 156** Slide forward on the left foot and take up a left walking stance. Perform a high block using left double forearm.

21 **Fig. 157** Pull the left foot back into right L-stance and perform a left side punch.

㉒ Fig. 158 Bring your right knee up and forward and thrust your right foot out in a side piercing kick to the opponent's midsection.

㉓ Fig. 159 Drop the spent foot into a right walking stance and perform a high right double forearm block.

㉔ Fig. 160 Pull the right foot back into left L-stance and thrust out your right fist in a side punch.

25 **Fig. 161** Bring your left knee up and forward and thrust out your left foot in a middle side piercing kick.

26 **Fig. 162** *Above, right.* Drop the left foot into a right L-stance and perform a middle guarding forearm block.

27 **Fig. 163** Slowly, deliberately slide your left foot forward and bring your right hand back, palm facing upward. Extend the left arm and then turn the palm downward.

27 *cont.* **Fig. 164** Twist your hips anti-clockwise into a left low stance while performing a right palm pressing block.

28 **Fig. 165** Step forward with your right foot into left L-stance and perform a middle forearm guarding block.

29 **Fig. 166** Slowly and deliberately slide your right foot diagonally forward. Bring your left arm back with the palm turned upward and fingers extended. Fully extend your right arm and turn the palm down to the floor. Then twist your hips clockwise into right low stance while performing a left palm pressing block.

㉚ Fig. 167 Draw the left foot to the right and turn anti-clockwise.

㉚ cont. Fig. 168 Take up a closed stance as you pull your left fist back to your hip and take the right, palm downward across your chest. Move slowly and smoothly in what is a postural action.

31 **Fig. 169** Slide your right foot forward and take up fixed stance. At the same time, perform U-shaped block.

32 **Fig. 170** *Below, left.* Draw the right foot back to the left, lower your left hand and raise the right.

32 *cont.* **Fig. 171** *Below.* Slide your left foot into fixed stance and perform a second U-shaped block with *kihap*.

Draw the left foot back and resume closed ready stance 'B'.

One-step sparring
(ilbo matsoki)

One-step sparring begins at 4th kup level. This is a very useful half-way house between the increasing realism of the prearranged sparring practised so far and the unprogrammed exchange of free sparring. The attacker selects any single technique without prearranging it with the defender, so the latter must be both nimble and skilled to deflect it. The defender then performs a decisive counter, or series of counters, all of which are designed to exploit newly-gained skills. Each defence must be performed to a left and right attack.

Unlike free sparring, where the choice of techniques is limited by considerations of safety, one-step sparring offers an opportunity to use any valid technique, including grappling. The sparring partners normally begin from parallel ready stance but after that, anything goes! The attacker is first to *kihap*; the defender responds. The following two sequences are intended simply to illustrate the level of skill required in formulating one-step sparring at this grade.

One-step sparring (1)

Fig. 172 The attacker slides his right foot forward and into middle right obverse punch. Step out with your left foot and deflect the punch with right outside knife hand.

Fig. 173 Lift your right knee to chamber position and thrust out middle side kick.

Fig. 174 Turn your hips clockwise and drop the spent foot into right walking stance. Thrust out left high reverse punch into the opponent's face and *kihap*.

One-step sparring (2)

Fig. 175 The attacker steps forward into right walking stance and performs middle obverse punch. Step back with your left foot into left L-stance and deflect the punch with an inward moving forearm block.

Fig. 176 Twist your hips clockwise and perform a high front elbow strike (*nopun palkup*) against the attacker's jaw.

Fig. 177 Quickly draw back your left arm, using this action to help power a right middle upset punch to the attacker's solar plexus.

Fig. 178 Complete the sequence by sharply straightening up, drawing back your left fist and performing rising elbow strike to the opponent's chin. *Kihap* at this point.

Free sparring

Effective free sparring is a requirement for this grade. You should now be showing a high level of control and a grasp of the concepts of timing and distance.

Destruction
(gyokpa)

Tae kwon-do has always tested the effectiveness of the many techniques in its syllabus by means of destruction, or 'breaking'. In this test, the material to be broken (usually wooden boards, reusable plastic boards, bricks or tiles) is held between the jaws of a wooden breaking horse (*gyokpa tul*). The breaking horse is a tall trestle-like structure capable of taking two sizes of material in its twin jaws. The TAGB favours the use of reusable plastic boards held together by an impact resistant joint. If sufficient impact energy is transmitted, the joint springs open and the two pieces of board fly apart. The board can then be reassembled by sliding the joints together again. There are two grades of impact resistance, the white boards requiring less impact than the black ones. One or several such boards can be fitted into the jaws of the breaking horse, to be broken with a single technique performed from either side.

Figs 179 and 180
For 4th kup, the requirement is that you break one white board with a hand technique of your choice and one white board with a foot technique of your choice. Position yourself near the horse and check your range and angle. Then perform the selected technique slowly, bringing your body weapon against the board. When you are ready, cock the technique, let out a *kihap* and hit the board hard.

Figs 181 and 182 You can test any technique in this way, though accuracy is of vital importance to avoid inadvertently striking the jaws of the horse instead of the board! Kicking techniques are particularly susceptible to accuracy faults and you should use only those you are competent in.

Note: on medical advice, the TAGB does not allow persons below the age of 16 years to take part in destruction testing. This is because the bones of their wrists, hands and feet may not be fully formed, in which case hard impacts might damage them.

Blue Belt (3rd kup)

3rd kup introduces two new strikes, three new kicks, three new blocks and a jumping X-block into the curriculum.

Flat fingertip thrust
(opun sonkut tulgi)

Fig. 183 Extended fingers are a weapon we first encountered in the 7th kup. This time, however, instead of the hand held vertically with thumb uppermost, the palm is turned down to the floor. This configuration allows the weapon to slip in through a narrow opening to strike the target. Slide into a left walking stance and draw your right fist back to the hip. Use both these actions to help power a left high thrust into the opponent's throat. The narrowness of the flat fingertip thrust allows it to slip in under the chin to attack the throat (be careful – this is a dangerous technique!).

Upset fingertip thrust
(dwijibun sonkut tulgi)

Fig. 184 Upset fingertip thrust is similar to the above except that it is delivered with the palm facing upward. Slide your left leg forward and into left walking stance, combining a pull back of your left arm with a thrust out of the right. Strike the opponent's groin. Your left hand acts as a guard but it can also block outward and down, should the need arise.

Vertical kick
(sewo chagi)

Vertical kick uses a pronounced circular action to bring the little toe edge of the vertical foot into the target. We encounter it in the one-step sparring sequence selected for this grade and it can be used against a variety of targets, but in this particular example it is serving to wipe the opponent's obverse punch out of the way, exposing him to a follow-up technique.

The attacker steps into right walking stance and performs a high obverse punch. Step back to set up your range and pick up your left foot. Keep it vertical as you sweep the foot up and out to the left, knocking his forearm to the side (see **fig. 234** on page 108).

Reverse hooking kick
(bandae dollyo goro chagi)

Reverse hooking kick is a sophisticated and relatively short range technique which lifts the heel high over obstacles (such as the shoulder) before hooking it back into the target. The heel is used to deliver the impact and obvious targets include the back of the head and kidneys. However, high versions of the kick require considerable hip flexibility.

The attacker steps forward into right walking stance and performs middle obverse punch. Step back with your left foot and grasp his wrist with your right hand. Keep hold of his wrist as you draw your foot into chamber position (see **fig. 241** on page 110). Note that the heel is at the same height as the knee, the left fist is in a guard position and the supporting foot has rotated outward.

Curl your heel over his shoulder and bring it sharply into the back of his head (see **fig. 242** on page 111). Then release your grip on his wrist and withdraw into a safe guarding posture.

Jumping side piercing kick
(twimyo yopcha jirugi)

In no other martial art do the jumping kicks reach such a degree of sophistication as they do in tae kwon-do. A jumping kick is one in which the foot weapon strikes the target while the supporting leg is clear of the floor. Sometimes jumping kicks are performed simply to gain height, otherwise they may be used to cover distance. Whichever is the case, they require a high degree of elastic strength in the leg muscles. Begin the kick as you are rising – not as you top out!

The final one-step sparring sequence selected as an example for this grade features a jumping side piercing kick.

The opponent steps into left walking stance and performs middle obverse punch. Draw back out of range into left vertical stance (see **fig. 244** on page 112).

Spring up and thrust the little toe edge of your right foot into the opponent's face, tucking your left leg up as the right knee straightens (see **fig. 245** on page 112). Keep control over your arms and aim to land in an effective stance.

Back strike to rear/low block
(dwitcha dung joomuk/ bakat palmok makgi)

Fig. 185 It isn't always possible to deal with an opponent standing conveniently in front of you and there may be times when you have to be able to hit hard and effectively regardless of the way you are facing. In this case, the opponent in front of you has launched a left front kick which you bat out of the way with a low block. Even as your left arm sweeps down, the right snaps up and back, striking the opponent's face with the back of your right fist. Practise generating power by arm and upper body movement alone.

X-fist pressing block
(kyocha joomuk noollo makgi)

Fig. 186 We encountered X-fist in the previous form when it was used against a descending technique. In this case, you slide into the opponent in left walking stance, turning your hips toward him and thrusting out both your fists from the hips. Your forearms cross each other and the opponent's shin is caught between them. A certain amount of forward lean is necessary and the arms should be thrust well out from the body. If this isn't done, the opponent's foot may reach your groin!

W-shaped block
(bakat palmok san makgi)

W-shaped block uses a large movement of the arms and body to deflect an incoming technique. Begin in sitting stance with your right side toward the opponent. Lift both your fists so the forearms are vertical and the upper arms horizontal.

Fig. 187 Even as he begins his attack, lift your left foot and move it quickly across the front of your body, bringing it down hard in a stamping action to concentrate force. Your whole body rotates through 180° and the little finger side of your left forearm knocks the opponent's side kick off course.

Double forearm pushing block
(doo palmok miro makgi)

As its name implies, pushing block unbalances the opponent by vigorously pushing his chosen technique away from you. Begin to slide your right foot forward and swing both arms out behind you. Both fists are turned so the palms face downward (see **fig. 207** on page 100).

Continue sliding forward into a right L-stance and perform low pushing block with a left double forearm (see **fig. 208** on page 100) so the opponent's incoming front kick is jolted to the side.

Jump into X-block in X-stance

Fig. 188 The opponent is armed with a staff which he swings violently against your legs. Avoid it by jumping high into the air, drawing your elbows right back.

Fig. 189 Land lightly in right X-stance and thrust both fists out against the opponent's front kick.

Toi Gye

Toi Gye is the pen name of the 16th century scholar Yi Wang who was regarded as an authority on neo-Confucianism. The diagram of the 37 movements represents both the calligraphy for 'scholar' and his birthplace on the 37° latitude.

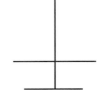

❶ **Fig. 190** Begin from closed ready stance 'B' with your right fist clasped in your left hand at belt height. Step out to the side with your left foot into right L-stance and perform middle side block with your left inner forearm.

❷ **Fig. 191** Turn your hips clockwise and both lift and open your right hand, turning the palm down to the floor. Rotate your left fist so the palm is facing downward.

❷ *cont.* **Fig. 192** Slide your left foot forward and turn your hips forward as you take up walking stance. Thrust out your right hand in an upset fingertip strike while drawing the left fist back to your right shoulder.

❸ **Fig. 193** *Above, right.* Draw back your left foot and twist your hips clockwise. Fold your right elbow across the outside of your left forearm, closing the right hand into a fist.

❸ *cont.* **Fig. 194** Continue turning clockwise and bring your left foot to the right, forming closed stance. Slowly and smoothly perform a high side strike with the right fist and a low block with the left forearm.

❹ **Fig. 195** Turn to your right and slide your right foot forward so you take up left L-stance. Draw back your left fist and turn it palm upward, using this action to help power a middle side block with your right inner forearm.

❺ **Fig. 196** *Above, right.* Slide your right foot forward into walking stance and thrust out your left arm in a low upset fingertip strike. At the same time, draw your right side fist back to your left shoulder.

❻ **Fig. 197** Draw back your right foot, turn anti-clockwise and form closed stance. At the same time, smoothly and deliberately perform a high strike with your left fist and a low block with the right forearm.

❼ **Fig. 198** Slide your left foot diagonally forward and to the left, and turn your hips to the right, drawing both fists back to your hips.

❼ *cont.* **Fig. 199** *Above, right.* Turn your hips strongly anti-clockwise into left walking stance, using this action to help perform pressing block with X-fist.

❽ **Fig. 200** Withdraw your blocking arms and quickly thrust them back out in a twin fist vertical punch.

9 **Fig. 201** *Far left.* Maintain your hand position as you bring your right knee up to perform a middle front snap kick.

10 **Fig. 202** *Left.* Drop the spent foot carefully forward and take up right walking stance. Use the energy of your motion to help power a middle obverse punch.

11 **Fig. 203** *Right.* Pull your right fist back to the hip and at the same time thrust out a middle reverse punch with your left fist. The obverse/reverse punches follow each other in quick succession.

12 **Fig. 204** *Far right.* Slowly draw your left foot to the right and turn to the left to form closed stance. Draw both fists to your hips.

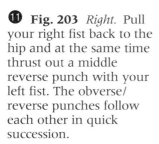

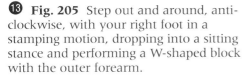

13 **Fig. 205** Step out and around, anti-clockwise, with your right foot in a stamping motion, dropping into a sitting stance and performing a W-shaped block with the outer forearm.

14 **Fig. 206** Swing your left foot out, up and around in a stamping motion, turning clockwise and dropping into a second sitting stance. Perform a second W-shaped block with the outer forearm.

15 Continue turning clockwise as you swing your left foot around in a stamping motion and drop into a third sitting stance. Perform a third W-shaped block with your outer forearm.

16 Swing your right foot around in a stamping motion, turning anti-clockwise and dropping into a fourth sitting stance. Perform a W-shaped block with your outer forearm.

17 Swing your left foot out and around in a stamping motion, turning clockwise and dropping into a fifth sitting stance. Perform a W-shaped block with your outer forearm.

18 Swing your left foot out and around in a stamping motion, turning clockwise and dropping into a sixth sitting stance. Perform W-shaped block with your outer forearm.

⑲ Fig. 207 *Far left.* Bring your right foot to the left and swing both arms out behind you. Both fists are turned so the palms face downward.

⑲ *cont.* Fig. 208 *Left.* Slide forward into a right L-stance and perform low pushing block with a left double forearm.

⑳ Fig. 209 *Right.* Slide your left foot forward into walking stance and reach up with both hands as though to grab the opponent's head.

㉑ Fig. 210 *Far right.* Pull the imaginary opponent's head down and bring your right knee sharply up and into his face.

22 **Fig. 211** Drop your right foot close to the left and turn anti-clockwise, trailing both hands palm downward behind you.

22 *cont.* **Fig. 212** Slide your left foot out into right L-stance and perform a middle knife hand guarding block.

23 **Fig. 213** *Above, right.* Don't move your hands as you perform a left low snap kick.

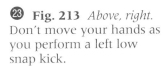

24 **Fig. 214** Carefully set down the spent kicking foot into left walking stance, using the energy of your landing to thrust out your left hand in a high flat fingertip configuration.

㉕ **Fig. 215** Step forward with your right foot into a left L-stance and perform middle knife hand guarding block.

㉖ **Fig. 216** Keep your arms still as you lift your right knee and perform low front snap kick.

㉗ **Fig. 217** *Above, right.* Carefully drop the spent right foot into walking stance, using the energy of your moving body to help power a high thrust with the right flat fingertips.

㉘ **Fig. 218** Draw the right foot back and twist clockwise. The palm of your left fist is brought close to your face and your right fist is to the outside, with the palm turned downward.

28 *cont.* **Fig. 219** *Far left.* Look over your right shoulder as you slide your right foot out and take up right L-stance. At the same time, perform a high strike with your right fist and a low block with the left forearm.

29 **Fig. 220** *Left.* Twist anti-clockwise and jump forward, drawing your elbows back.

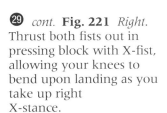

29 *cont.* **Fig. 221** *Right.* Thrust both fists out in pressing block with X-fist, allowing your knees to bend upon landing as you take up right X-stance.

30 **Fig. 222** *Far right.* Slide your right foot forward and trail both your arms to the left, palms facing downward.

30 *cont.* **Fig. 223** Twist your hips clockwise and transfer your weight forward into walking stance, using this action to help power a high block with right double forearm.

31 **Fig. 224** *Above, right.* Then draw back the left foot, turning clockwise again. Open your hands and bring the left hand close to your right ear while extending the right with the palm turned downward.

31 *cont.* **Fig. 225** Slide your left foot forward into right L-stance and perform a low guarding block with knife hand.

32 **Fig. 226** Slide your left foot further forward and take up walking stance. As you do this, perform a right middle circular block with your inner forearm.

33 **Fig. 227** *Above, right.* Bring your left foot to the right and continue to turn your hips clockwise. Bring your right palm near your left ear and extend the left. Then slide your right foot forward into left L-stance and perform low guarding block with knife hand.

34 **Fig. 228** Slide your right foot further forward into walking stance and perform circular block with your left inner forearm.

③⑤ **Fig. 229** Twist your hips strongly to the left. Your left fist turns palm down across your upper chest while the right trails palm down.

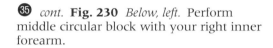

③⑤ *cont.* **Fig. 230** *Below, left.* Perform middle circular block with your right inner forearm.

③⑥ **Fig. 231** *Below.* Twist your hips to the right and perform a further circular block with your left inner forearm.

37 **Fig. 232** Twist your hips to the front and allow the right foot to slide forward.

37 *cont.* **Fig. 233** *Below.* Drop into a sitting stance, thrust out a right middle punch and *kihap*.

Draw the right foot back and resume ready stance once more.

One-step sparring

One-step sparring continues with more advanced responses to a single attack. The following three examples are intended to indicate the level of skill required in formulating one-step sparring at this grade.

One-step sparring (3)

Fig. 234 The attacker steps into right walking stance and performs high obverse punch. Step back to set up your range and sweep his forearm to the side with a vertical kick.

Fig. 235 *Above, right.* Drop your spent left foot so as to set up a following snap kick into the attacker's groin.

Fig. 236 Don't set your right foot down. Lift the knee and point it at the opponent's face.

Fig. 237 Perform high right turning kick into the side of the opponent's head.

Fig. 238 *Above, right.* Again, don't set the foot down. Take it across your body and point your right heel at the target.

Fig. 239 Thrust your right foot out in a high side piercing kick to the opponent's chin. *Kihap* at this point, then withdraw your foot and set it down.

One-step sparring (4)

Fig. 240 The attacker steps forward into right walking stance and performs middle obverse punch. Step back with your left foot and grasp the opponent's wrist with your right hand. Draw him forward and perform right side piercing kick to his ribs.

Fig. 241 Keep hold of his wrist as you draw your foot back into chamber position.

Fig. 242 The opponent is now fairly close to you, so use high section reverse hooking kick into the back of his head.

Fig. 243 Maintain your grip on his arm as you set your right foot down and perform a front elbow strike. *Kihap* at this point.

One-step sparring (5)

Fig. 244 The opponent steps into left walking stance and performs middle obverse punch. Draw back out of range into left vertical stance.

Fig. 245 Spring up and thrust the little toe edge of your right foot into the opponent's face in a jumping side piercing kick. Land and take up an effective guarding posture.

Free sparring

Free sparring is a requirement for this grade, and by now you should be showing a knowledge of basic tactics, leading to a polished performance with few wasted techniques.

Destruction

The destruction requirements for 3rd kup are that you should break a single white board with a hand and a foot technique of your choice. Each break must be performed on both left and right sides.

Red Belt (2nd kup)

2nd kup introduces a new stance, two new hand attacks, two blocks and a response to having your wrist grabbed by the opponent.

Closed ready stance 'C'
(moa junbi sogi 'C')
Closed ready stance 'C' has the feet together and the open hands crossed in front of the groin. Turn your palms toward your body and have the left hand overlie the right (see **fig. 252** on page 116).

Upward punch
(ollyo jirugi)

Fig. 246 Upward punch is a short range technique that swings around and up into the target. Impact is made with knuckles turned downward. Take up left L-stance and deflect the opponent's left punch. Your right hand comes across your upper body and the left swings around and up in an uppercut to the opponent's chin.

Descending knife hand strike
(sonkal naeryo taerigi)

Fig. 247 Descending knife hand strike drops vertically down onto the target (in this case, the opponent's collar bone). Turn your body sideways-on to the opponent in vertical stance and move the strike up and across your chest, lifting high before descending onto the target.

Palm pushing block
(sonbadak miro makgi)

Fig. 248 Palm pushing block thrusts the palm of your hand into the opponent's chest, preventing him from closing with you and positioning him for a punch. Your right fist is ready on the hip.

Low block with outer forearm/ middle block with left inner forearm
(bakat palmok makgi/ an palmok makgi)

Fig. 249 This combination of blocks deals with simultaneous attacks by two opponents – it isn't often they politely wait their turn to attack you in real life! Parry one opponent's front kick by driving your right forearm down in a low block. At the same time, swing your left forearm up to knock the other opponent's middle punch off course. Be prepared to switch between the two.

Release from wrist grab

Fig. 250 This release features in the pattern Hwa Rang which follows. In it, you have attempted right obverse punch but the opponent has stepped back and grabbed your wrist. Respond by sliding your back foot up and wrapping your left fingers around your right knuckles.

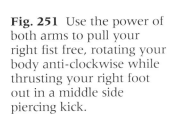

Fig. 251 Use the power of both arms to pull your right fist free, rotating your body anti-clockwise while thrusting your right foot out in a middle side piercing kick.

Hwa Rang

Hwa Rang is the name given to an army of young warriors from the Silla Dynasty of Korea. They were first mentioned in AD 600, and over the years they gradually became a significant force in the unification of Korea's three kingdoms. Hwa Rang means 'Flowering Youth', and comprises 29 movements which refer to the 29th Infantry Division where tae kwon-do developed. Those movements are arranged in the following pattern:

Fig. 252 Begin from closed ready stance 'C'.

❶ **Fig. 253** Slide your left foot to the left and drop into sitting stance. As you do, thrust out the palm of your left hand in a middle pushing block.

❷ **Fig. 254** Pull back your left hand and spasm-close it into a fist on your right hip. Use this action to help thrust out a right middle punch.

❸ **Fig. 255** *Above, right.* Quickly draw back your right fist and thrust out a left middle punch. The two punches follow each other in quick succession.

❹ **Fig. 256** Swivel clockwise and take up left L-stance. Perform twin forearm block.

117

❺ **Fig. 257** Bring your right side fist to your left shoulder as you drop your left fist and then swing it up into an upward punch.

❻ **Fig. 258** *Below, left.* Draw back your left fist and simultaneously slide forward with both feet as you thrust out a right middle punch using fixed stance.

❼ **Fig. 259** *Below.* Take your left arm across your chest and turn the fist palm downward. Open your right hand and bring it down across your lower body.

7 *cont.* **Fig. 260** Draw your right foot back into left vertical stance and pull your left fist back to the hip. Your right knife hand passes the front of your left shoulder and carries on into a downward strike.

8 **Fig. 261** *Above, right.* Step forward with your left foot, draw back your right hand and perform obverse punch to mid-section with the left fist.

9 **Fig. 262** Draw back your left foot and turn your hips 90° anti-clockwise. Make ready to perform a low block with the left forearm.

9 *cont.* **Fig. 263** Slide your left foot forward into walking stance and perform low block.

10 **Fig. 264** *Above, right.* Step forward on your right foot, draw back your left fist and simultaneously punch with the right fist.

11 **Fig. 265** Draw up your left foot until your heels touch. Take your left hand forward and envelop the right fist. You may slightly bend your right elbow.

11 *cont.* **Fig. 266** Pull your hands back anti-clockwise and thrust your right heel out in a middle side piercing kick.

12 **Fig. 267** Drop your right foot into left L-stance, pull your left hand back and perform a middle side strike with right knife hand.

13 **Fig. 268** Step forward with your left foot into walking stance, pull back your knife hand and thrust out left middle obverse punch.

14 **Fig. 269** Take another step forward, this time into right walking stance and perform right middle obverse punch.

15 **Fig. 270** *Above, right.* Turn your body 270° anti-clockwise, sliding your left foot across and opening your right fist so the palm is turned away from you.

15 *cont.* **Fig. 271** Step out with your left foot into right L-stance and take up a left middle knife hand guarding block.

16 **Fig. 272** Step forward into right walking stance, drawing back your left hand and performing a right middle fingertip thrust. The back of your left hand is just below your right elbow.

17 **Fig. 273** *Above, right.* Draw back your left and right feet, and prepare your hands to perform knife hand guarding block.

17 *cont.* **Fig. 274** Drop your weight over your right foot and perform left middle knife hand guarding block from right L-stance.

18 **Fig. 275** Transfer weight over your leading left foot and perform a high right foot turning kick.

19 **Fig. 276** *Above, right.* Drop your spent foot forward and perform a second high turning kick, this time with the left foot.

19 *cont.* **Fig. 277** Drop the spent kick into right L-stance and perform middle knife hand guarding block.

20 **Fig. 278** Swivel your hips 90° anti-clockwise and allow the left to slide. Bring both forearms up and across your upper chest and face. Look left.

20 *cont.* **Fig. 279** Slide your left foot out and perform low block from left walking stance.

21 **Fig. 280** Draw back your left foot and blocking fist, using this action to help thrust out a right middle punch.

㉒ **Fig. 281** Step forward into left L-stance, pulling back your right fist and performing middle punch with the left.

㉓ **Fig. 282** Step forward into right L-stance, pulling back your left fist and performing middle punch with the right.

㉔ **Fig. 283** Twist your hips clockwise and bring both your fists back.

24 *cont.* **Fig. 284** Twist your hips back to the front and allow your left foot to slide into walking stance. Thrust both fists out in an X-fist pressing block.

25 **Fig. 285** Bring your right foot forward and turn your hips 180° anti-clockwise. Take your right fist across the front of your chest.

㉕ *cont.* **Fig. 286**
Continue sliding the right foot forward and drop into a right L-stance. Thrust your right elbow out to the side.

㉖ **Fig. 287** Draw back your left foot and turn anti-clockwise, taking your left arm across the front of your chest while extending the right.

㉖ *cont.* **Fig. 288**
Continue turning 90° anti-clockwise into closed stance, and low block with your left forearm while simultaneously performing middle block with your right inner forearm.

27 **Fig. 289** Now take your right arm down into a low block as you middle block with your left inner forearm.

28 **Fig. 290** Step forward with your left foot into right L-stance and perform a middle knife hand guarding block.

㉙ Fig. 291 Draw the left foot back to the right, turn clockwise and slide the right forward into left L-stance. Perform middle knife hand guarding block and *kihap*.

Draw your right foot to the left and resume closed ready stance 'C'.

Sparring

You will be expected to show advanced examples of three-step semi-free sparring, two-step sparring and one-step sparring. Additionally, you will be required to demonstrate skill in free sparring.

Destruction

The destruction requirements for 2nd kup are that you should break two white boards with a hand and a foot technique of your choice. Each break must be performed on both left and right sides.

Red Belt (1st kup)

1st kup introduces two new strikes, two new kicks, two blocks and a grab/jump/spin .

High front knife hand strike
(sonkal anuro taerigi)
Inward knife hand strike uses the little finger edge of the hand in a palm upward configuration to attack the side of the opponent's neck.

Fig. 292 As you step into right forward stance, the opponent attempts descending knife hand strike against your left collar bone. Deflect his strike with your left knife hand guard while simultaneously swinging your right knife hand around horizontally and into the side of his neck. Simultaneous moves like this, where blocks and counters are performed concurrently, are a feature of the more sophisticated tae kwon-do you are now practising.

High reverse knife hand strike
(sonkal dung taerigi)

Reverse knife hand strike uses the thumb- or 'ridge'-side of your hand in a horizontal strike to such targets as the opponent's neck.

Fig. 293 Slide your left foot into left walking stance and swing your right hand around and into the side of the opponent's neck. Your left hand swings under your right elbow in a defensive position and as a reaction to the in-swinging right hand.

Jumping high side piercing kick
(twimyo yopcha jirugi)

You have already practised this kick in a direct jumping version. However, in this case, the kick makes use of an accelerator step to increase the range and height and the kick comes from the trailing foot, so there is marked rotation in the air.

Begin from right L-stance and middle knife hand guarding block (see **fig. 303** on page 139).

Step quickly through with your right foot (see **fig. 304** on page 140).

Lift your left knee high as though you were stepping onto a high chair (see **fig. 305** on page 140).

Use your lifting left knee to 'lever' yourself into the air and perform flying side piercing kick with your right foot. Your left foot must be clear of the floor as the right hits the target (see **fig. 306** on page 141).

Land and take up left L-stance while performing a knife hand guarding block.

Back piercing kick (reverse side kick)
(dwitcha jirugi)

Back piercing kick uses the little toe edge of the foot (the 'footsword') in a backward travelling kick.

You have just performed a high right turning kick (see **fig. 314** on page 145) and the spent foot has been dropped slightly in front of and to the side of your left foot. Continue the rotational motion of the turning kick by pivoting on your right foot and looking over your left shoulder (see **fig. 315** on page 145). Pick up your left foot and thrust it out directly (see **fig. 316** on page 146), retrieving it afterwards and setting it down in an effective guarding posture. Keep control over your arms.

Middle side X-checking block with knife hand
(kyocha sonkal momchau makgi)

This is a checking block which is useful against turning or reverse turning kicks. The elbows are first withdrawn, then the two knife hands are thrust out in an X-configuration, the one overlying and reinforcing the other.

Use middle side X-block as you turn toward the opponent. Draw back your elbows and then thrust your open hands across in an X-configuration to block the opponent's turning kick (see **fig. 336** on page 155).

Twin upward palm block
(doo sonbadak ollyo makgi)

Twin upward palm block uses the same principle as the single version we practised for 6th kup. This time, however, both the opponent's forearms are deflected upward.

Fig. 294 Step forward with your left foot into walking stance and bring your palms under the opponent's forearms, lifting them and exposing the groin to a follow-up attack.

Block, jump and spin

This is taken from the pattern Choong Moo. Your imaginary opponent is armed with a staff, so slide your right foot forward into fixed stance and perform U-shaped block. Then jump and turn anti-clockwise in the air to confuse the opponent. Land in left L-stance on the same spot you jumped from. Make safe on landing by performing a middle knife hand guarding block.

Choong Moo

Choong Moo was the name given to the Yi Dynasty admiral, Yi Sun-Sin. In AD 1592, he is reputed to have invented the world's first armoured ship which was the precursor of today's submarine. The reason this pattern ends with a left hand attack is to symbolise his regrettable death, having no chance to show his full potential through the constraints of his loyalty to the king. Choong Moo consists of 30 moves arranged in the following pattern:

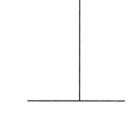

The pattern begins from parallel ready stance, with your feet a shoulder-width apart and facing forward, and your hands closed into fists.

❶ Fig. 295 Slide your left foot to the left, turn your hips anti-clockwise and take up right L-stance. Perform twin knife hand block.

135

❷ **Fig. 296** Step forward with your right foot into right walking stance. Perform a high inward knife hand strike with your right hand and move your left hand to just in front of your forehead.

❸ **Fig. 297** Pivot 180° clockwise on your left foot and draw the right foot back.

❸ *cont.* **Fig. 298** Complete your clockwise rotation and slide your right foot forward into left L-stance. Perform a middle knife hand guarding block.

❹ **Fig. 299** Step forward with your left foot into left walking stance. Perform high thrust with the flat fingertips of the left hand.

❺ Fig. 300 Draw your left foot to the left and pivot 90° in an anti-clockwise direction, taking up right L-stance. Perform middle knife hand guarding block.

❻ Fig. 301 Transfer bodyweight over your left foot and twist your upper body clockwise by 180°. Lift your right knee and take up left bending ready stance 'A'.

138

❼ Fig. 302 Thrust your right foot out in a middle side piercing kick.

❽ Fig. 303 Drop the spent foot and turn 180° anti-clockwise into right L-stance while performing a middle knife hand guarding block.

139

9 **Fig. 304** Step quickly through with your right foot, using the step as an accelerator.

9 *cont.* **Fig. 305** Lift your left knee as though you were stepping onto a high chair.

❾ *cont.* **Fig. 306** Use your lifting left knee to 'lever' yourself into the air and perform flying side piercing kick with your right foot.

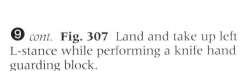

❾ *cont.* **Fig. 307** Land and take up left L-stance while performing a knife hand guarding block.

❿ Fig. 308 Slide the left foot across as you turn 90° anti-clockwise and cross your forearms.

❿ *cont.* **Fig. 309** Complete anti-clockwise rotation and take up right L-stance while performing low block with your left forearm.

⓫ Fig. 310 Slide your left foot forward into left walking stance and reach forward with both hands, as though to grab the opponent's head.

⓬ Fig. 311 Pull the imaginary opponent's head down and perform right knee strike to his solar plexus.

⑬ **Fig. 312** Drop the right foot to the left, then twist your hips 180° anticlockwise, trailing the right open hand as you do so.

⑬ *cont.* **Fig. 313** Slide your left foot into left walking stance and perform high front strike with right reverse knife hand, bringing the left hand under your right elbow.

14 **Fig. 314** Quickly bring your right knee forward and perform a high turning kick with your right foot.

15 **Fig. 315** Drop the spent foot close to your left foot and twist your upper body anti-clockwise to look behind you.

15 *cont.* **Fig. 316**
Without pausing, go on to perform a middle reverse side kick with your left foot.

16 **Fig. 317** Lower the spent left foot and take up left L-stance. Perform middle forearm guarding block.

⓱ Fig. 318 Pivot 45° on your right foot, performing a middle turning kick with your left foot.

⓲ Fig. 319 Drop the left foot close by the right and turn your body clockwise. Open your hands.

18 *cont.* **Fig. 320** Slide your right foot forward into fixed stance and perform U-shaped block.

19 Fig. 321 Jump and turn anti-clockwise in the air.

19 *cont.* **Fig. 322** Land in left L-stance on the same spot you jumped from. Perform middle knife hand guarding block.

20 **Fig. 323** Step into left walking stance and perform low thrust with upset right fingertips.

21 **Fig. 324** Pull your bodyweight back over your right foot forming right L-stance and look over your right shoulder.

㉑ *cont.* **Fig. 325** Perform high strike with right back fist and a low block with your left forearm.

㉒ **Fig. 326** Step forward into right walking stance and perform right middle thrust with the straight fingertips of your right hand.

㉓ **Fig. 327** Spin anti-clockwise on your right foot, drawing the left foot to it. Trail your fists.

㉓ *cont.* **Fig. 328** Slide the left foot forward into walking stance and perform high block with left double forearm.

㉔ **Fig. 329** Step forward with your right foot and draw your right fist back.

㉔ *cont.* **Fig. 330**
Continue forward with your right foot and turn anti-clockwise into sitting stance. Perform middle front block with your right outer forearm.

24 *cont.* **Fig. 331** Look to your right and cross your forearms. Pull back your left fist and perform high side strike with your right fist.

25 **Fig. 332** Transfer your weight over your left foot and twist your hips strongly through 180° in an anti-clockwise direction. Lift your right knee.

㉕ *cont.* **Fig. 333**
Perform a middle right side piercing kick.

㉖ Fig. 334 Lower the spent foot.

26 *cont.* **Fig. 335** Bring your left foot forward and perform a left middle side piercing kick.

27 **Fig. 336** Drop your left foot and pivot clockwise into left L-stance. Perform a middle side checking block with X knife hand.

28 **Fig. 337** Step forward with your left foot into walking stance and perform twin upward palm block.

29 **Fig. 338** Turn clockwise and slide your right foot across, crossing your forearms in front of your upper body.

29 *cont.* **Fig. 339** *Right.* Twist your hips powerfully to the right, sliding your right foot into walking stance. Perform a rising block with your right forearm.

30 Fig. 340 *Left.* Strongly pull back your right fist, using this action to help power a middle left reverse punch. *Kihap* at this point.

Draw back your left foot and resume ready stance.

Sparring
The requirement for this grade is clear evidence of a continuing improvement in the skilful usage of techniques and tactics.

Destruction
The destruction requirements for 1st kup are that you should break two white boards with a hand and a foot technique of your choice. Each break must be performed on both left and right sides.

Appendix
Korean terminology

Tae kwon-do is a Korean martial art, so Korean terminology is used. Learning this means you will be able to train all over the world and understand what is being asked of you.

About turn *Dwiyro torro*
Attention! *Charyot*
Attention stance *Charyot sogi*

Back fist *Dung joomuk*
Back fist strike *Dung joomuk taerigi*
Back kick *Dwit chagi*
Back piercing kick *Dwitcha jirugi*
Back strike to rear *Dwitcha dung joomuk*
Backwards *Dwiyro kaggi*
Ball of foot *Ap kumchi*
Begin *Si jak*
Belt *Ti*
Bending ready stance *Guburyo junbi sogi*
Bow *Kyong Ye*

Circular block *Dollimyo makgi*
Closed ready stance *Moa junbi sogi*

Descending knife hand strike *Sonkal naeryo taerigi*
Destruction *Gyokpa*

Dismiss *Haessan*
Double forearm block *Doo palmok makgi*
Double forearm pushing block *Doo palmok miro makgi*

Eight *Yodoll*

Fingertips *Sonkut*
Five *Dasaul*
Fixed stance *Gojung sogi*
Flat fingertip thrust *Opun sonkut tulgi*
Footsword *Balkal*
Forearm *Palmok*
Forefist *Ap joomuk*
Forwards *Apro kaggi*
Four *Neth*
Four-directional punch *Sajo jirugi*
Free sparring *Jayoo matsoki*
Front elbow strike *Palkup*
Front kick *Ap chagi*
Front rising kick *Apcha olligi*

Guarding block *Daebi makgi*

Heel *Dwikumchi*
High front elbow strike *Nopun palkup*
High front knife hand strike *Sonkal anuro taerigi*
High reverse knife hand strike *Sonkal dung taerigi*
High-section *Nopunde*

Inner forearm *An palmok*
Inner forearm block *An palmok makgi*
Instructor *Sabum*
Inward *Anaero*
Inward knife hand strike *Anuro sonkal taerigi*

Jumping side piercing kick *Twimyo yopcha jirugi*

Kick *Chagi*
Knee strike *Moorup*
Knife hand *Sonkal*
Knife hand guarding block *Sonkal daebi makgi*
Knife hand strike *Sonkal taerigi*

L-stance *Niunja sogi*
Left *Wen*
Low block *Bakat palmok makgi*
Low-section *Najunde*
Low stance *Nachuo sogi*

Middle block with left inner forearm *An palmok makgi*
Middle-section *Kaunde*
Middle side elbow strike *Yop palkup*
Middle side punch *Yop jirugi*
Middle side X-checking block with knife hand *Kyocha sonkal momchau makgi*

Nine *Ahop*

Obverse punch *Baro jirugi*
One *Hanna*
One-step sparring *Ilbo matsoki*
Outer forearm *Bakat palmok*
Outer forearm block *Bakat palmok makgi*
Outward *Bakaero*

Palm *Sonbadak*
Palm heel hooking block *Golcho makgi*
Palm pressing block *Sonbadak noollo makgi*
Palm pushing block *Sonbadak miro makgi*
Parallel stance *Narani sogi*
Pattern *Tul*

Ready *Chunbi*
Rear foot stance *Dwit bal sogi*

Return to ready stance *Barrol*
Reverse hooking kick *Bandae dollyo goro chagi*
Reverse knife hand block *Sonkal dung makgi*
Reverse punch *Bandae jirugi*
Reverse turning kick *Bandae dollyo chagi*
Right *Orun*
Rising block *Chookyo makgi*
Rising elbow strike *Wi palkup taerigi*
Rising X-block *Kyocha joomuk chookyo makgi*

Semi-free sparring *Ban jayoo matsoki*
Seven *Ilgop*
Shout *Kihap*
Side kick *Yop chagi*
Side rising kick *Yopcha olligi*
Sitting stance *Annun sogi*
Six *Yosaul*
Sparring *Matsoki*
Spear thrust *Sonkut tulgi*
Stop *Goman*
Straight *Son*
Student *Jeja*

Ten *Yoll*
Three *Seth*
Three-step sparring *Sambo matsoki*
Thrust *Tulgi*
Training hall *Dojang*
Training uniform *Dobok*
Turning kick *Dollyo chagi*
Twin forearm block *Sang palmok makgi*
Twin knife hand block *Sang sonkal makgi*

Twin straight forearm block *Sang sun palmok*
Twin upset punch *Sang dwijibo jirugi*
Twin upward palm block *Doo sonbadak ollyo makgi*
Twin vertical punch *Sang sewo jirugi*
Two *Dool*
Two-step sparring *Ibo matsoki*

U-shaped block *Mongdungi makgi*
Upset fingertip thrust *Dwijibun sonkut tulgi*
Upset punch *Dwijibo jirugi*
Upward palm block *Sonbadak ollyo makgi*
Upward punch *Ollyo jirugi*

Vertical kick *Sewo chagi*
Vertical stance *Soo jik sogi*

W-shaped block *Bakat palmok san makgi*
Waist block *Hori makgi*
Walking stance *Gunnun sogi*
Wedging block *Hechyo makgi*

X-fist pressing block *Kyocha joomuk noollo makgi*
X-stance *Kyocha sogi*

Index